5 FINGER
GERSHWIN CLASSICS

14 Timeless Songs Arranged for Piano With Optional Duet Accompaniments

TOM GEROU

Foreword

These timeless Gershwin classics have been arranged in traditional five-finger style, with the melody split between the left and right hands, and without key signatures in the solo part. Starting hand positions are illustrated above each piece. Fingerings that are outside of the noted five-finger positions are circled ① for easy identification. Dotted quarter notes, triplets and sixteenth-notes have been avoided. Leader lines in lyrics are omitted to avoid clutter. All of the melodic arrangements have optional duet accompaniments created to achieve a fuller, richer musical experience.

Contents

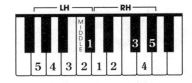

Bidin' My Time

Music and Lyrics by
GEORGE GERSHWIN and IRA GERSHWIN

Arr. by Tom Gerou

I'm bid - in' my time; 'cause that's the kind - a guy

I'm, while oth - er folks grow diz - zy I keep bus - y

Optional Duet Accompaniment (Play solo part 1 octave higher than written.)

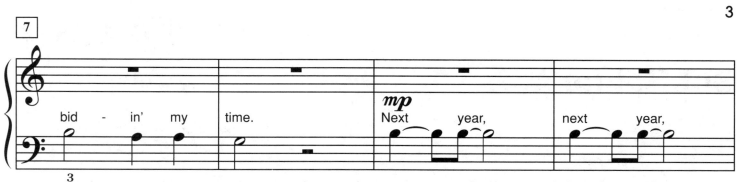

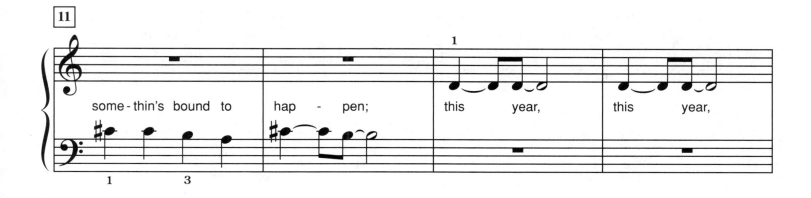

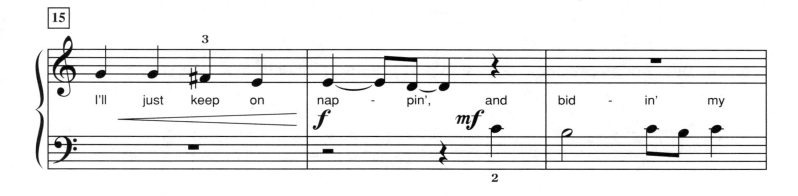

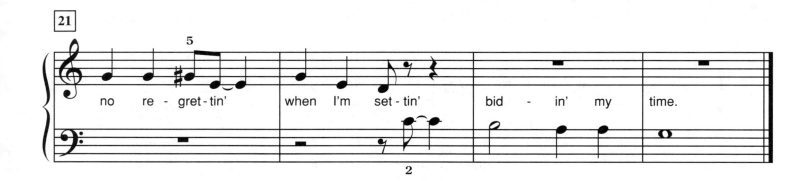

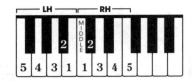

But Not for Me

Music and Lyrics by
GEORGE GERSHWIN and IRA GERSHWIN

Arr. by Tom Gerou

Moderately slow

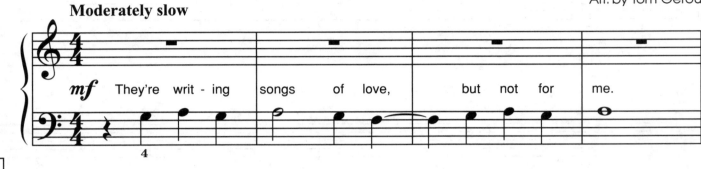

They're writ-ing songs of love, but not for me.

A luck-y star's a-bove, but not for me.

Optional Duet Accompaniment (Play solo part 1 octave higher than written.)

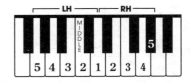

Embraceable You

Music and Lyrics by
GEORGE GERSHWIN and IRA GERSHWIN

Arr. by Tom Gerou

Optional Duet Accompaniment (Play solo part 1 octave higher than written.)

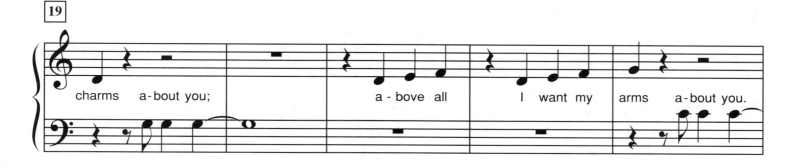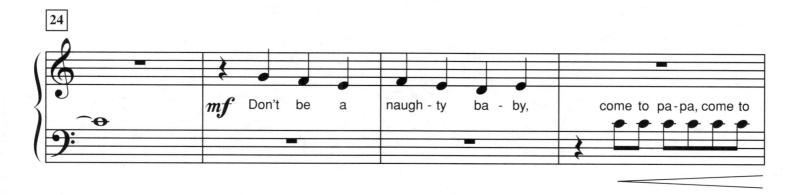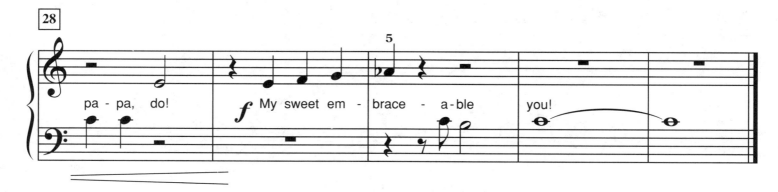

9 Just one look at you, my heart grew tip - sy in me; you and you a -

14 lone bring out the gyp - sy in me! *mp* I love all the man - y

19 charms a - bout you; a - bove all I want my arms a - bout you.

24 *mf* Don't be a naugh - ty ba - by, come to pa - pa, come to

28 pa - pa, do! *f* My sweet em - brace - a - ble you!

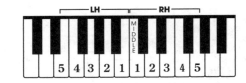

I've Got a Crush on You

Music and Lyrics by
GEORGE GERSHWIN and IRA GERSHWIN

Arr. by Tom Gerou

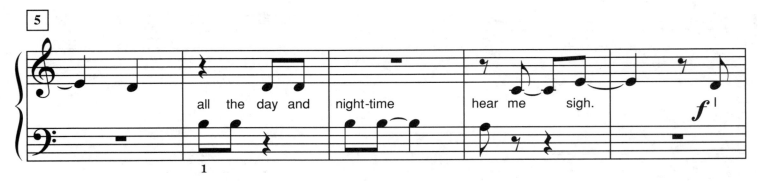

Optional Duet Accompaniment (Play solo part 1 octave higher than written.)

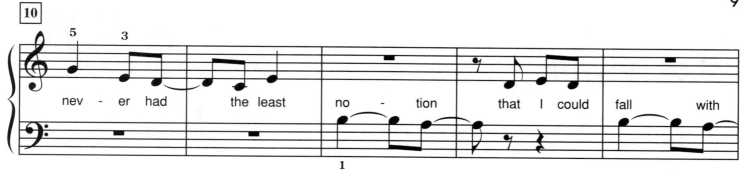

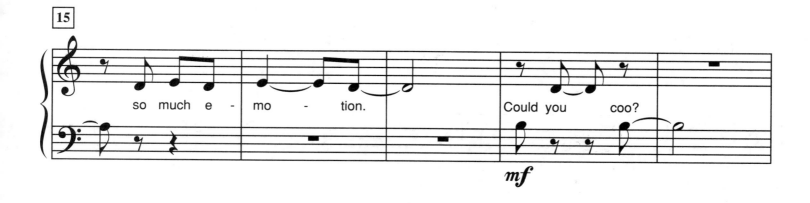

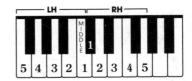

I Got Rhythm

Music and Lyrics by
GEORGE GERSHWIN and IRA GERSHWIN

Arr. by Tom Gerou

Quickly

Optional Duet Accompaniment (Play solo part 1 octave higher than written.)

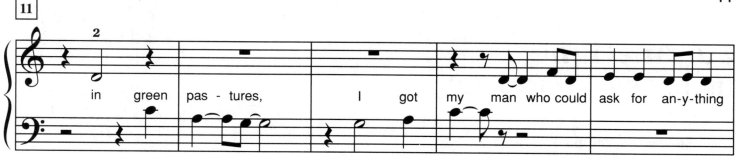

Summertime
(from *Porgy and Bess*)

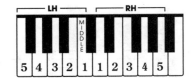

Music and Lyrics by
GEORGE GERSHWIN, IRA GERSHWIN and
DU BOSE and DOROTHY HEYWARD

Arr. by Tom Gerou

Slow swing tempo

Optional Duet Accompaniment (Play solo part 1 octave higher than written.)

Love Is Here to Stay

Music and Lyrics by
GEORGE GERSHWIN and IRA GERSHWIN

Arr. by Tom Gerou

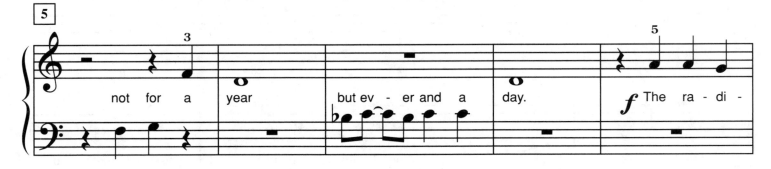

Optional Duet Accompaniment (Play solo part 1 octave higher than written.)

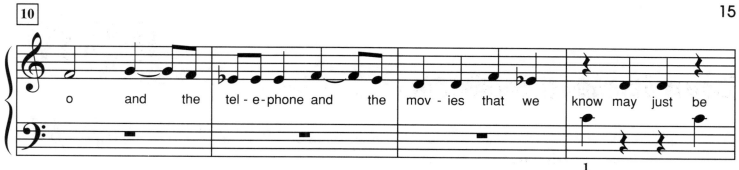

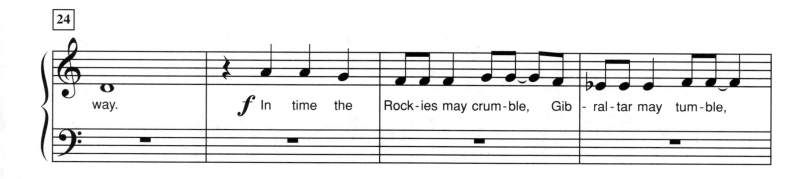

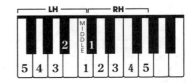

Somebody Loves Me

Music by GEORGE GERSHWIN
Lyrics by B. G. DeSYLVA and BALLARD MACDONALD

Arr. by Tom Gerou

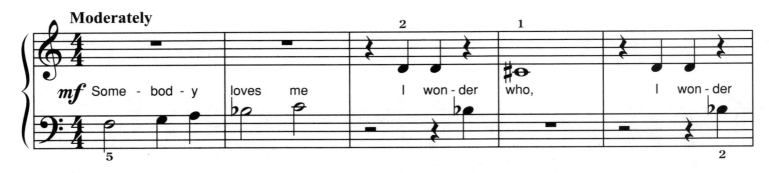

Optional Duet Accompaniment (Play solo part 1 octave higher than written.)

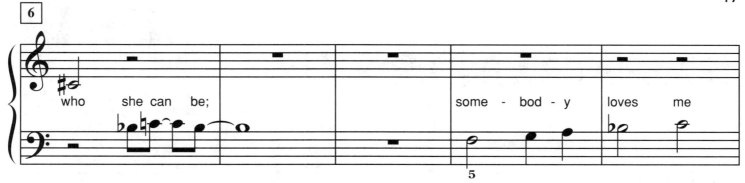

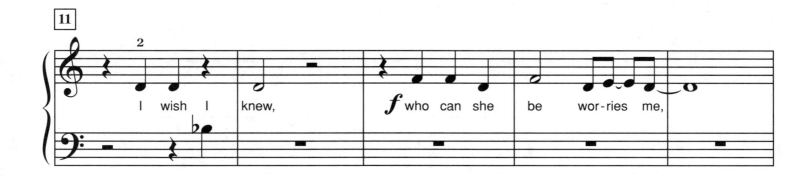

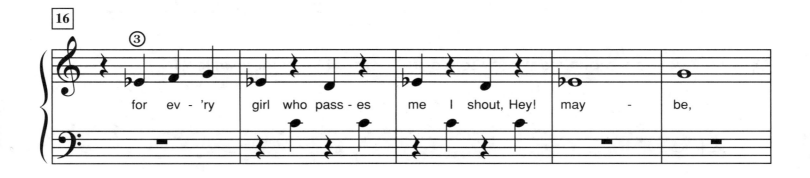

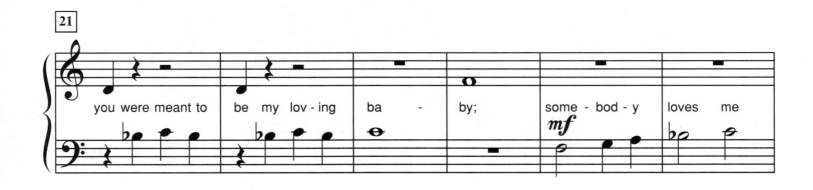

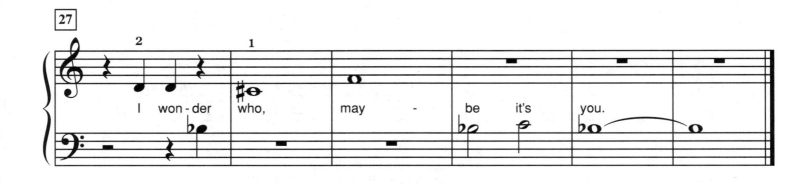

Someone to Watch Over Me

Music by GEORGE GERSHWIN
Lyrics by B. G. DeSYLVA and BALLARD MACDONALD

Arr. by Tom Gerou

Optional Duet Accompaniment (Play solo part 1 octave higher than written.)

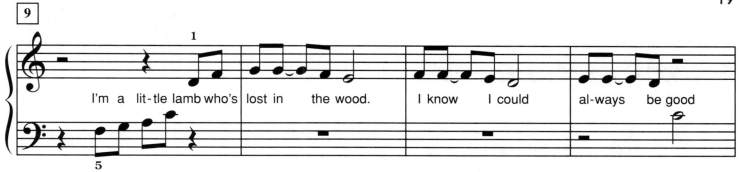

I'm a lit-tle lamb who's lost in the wood. I know I could al-ways be good

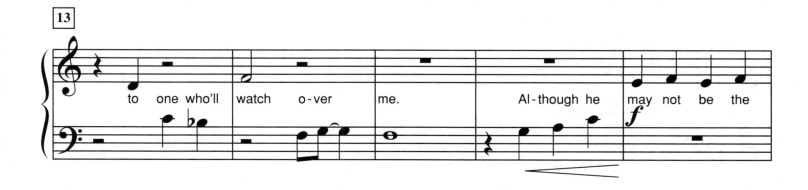

to one who'll watch o-ver me. Al-though he may not be the

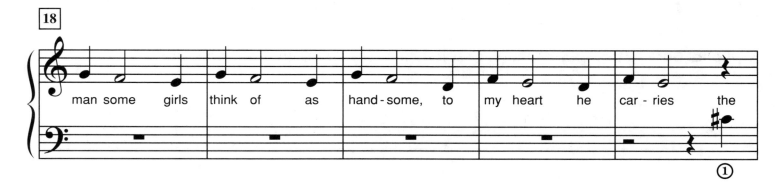

man some girls think of as hand-some, to my heart he car-ries the

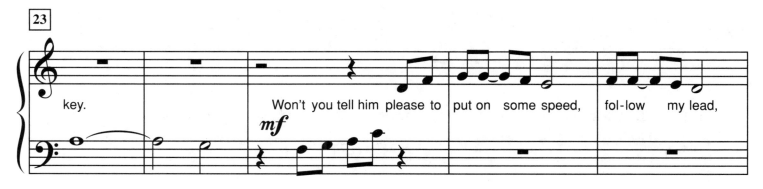

key. Won't you tell him please to put on some speed, fol-low my lead,

oh, how I need some-one to watch o-ver me.

Strike Up the Band!

Music and Lyrics by
GEORGE GERSHWIN and IRA GERSHWIN

Arr. by Tom Gerou

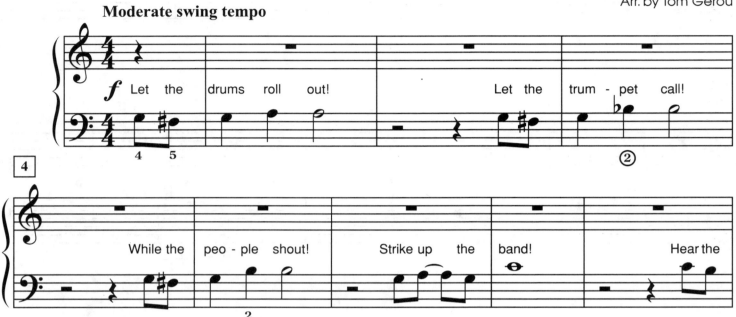

Moderate swing tempo

Let the drums roll out! — Let the trum - pet call!

While the peo - ple shout! — Strike up the band! — Hear the

Optional Duet Accompaniment (Play solo part 1 octave higher than written.)

Moderate swing tempo

cym - bals ring! Call-ing one and all to the mar-tial swing

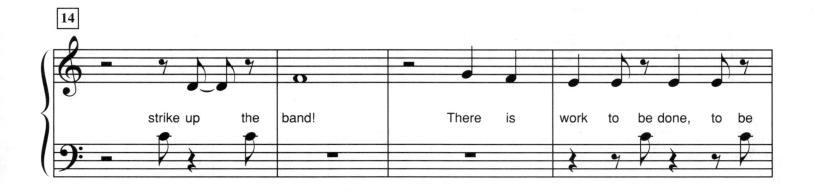

strike up the band! There is work to be done, to be

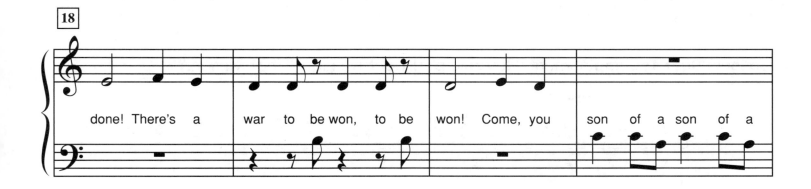

done! There's a war to be won, to be won! Come, you son of a son of a

gun! Take your stand! Fall in line, yea bo! Come a -

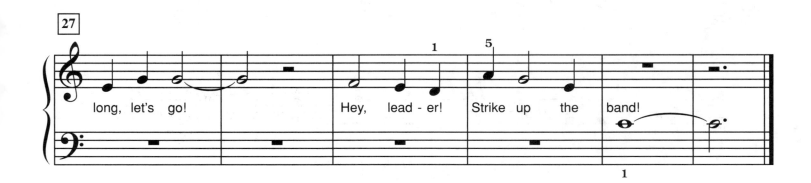

long, let's go! Hey, lead - er! Strike up the band!

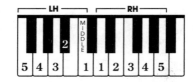

'S Wonderful

Music and Lyrics by
GEORGE GERSHWIN and IRA GERSHWIN

Arr. by Tom Gerou

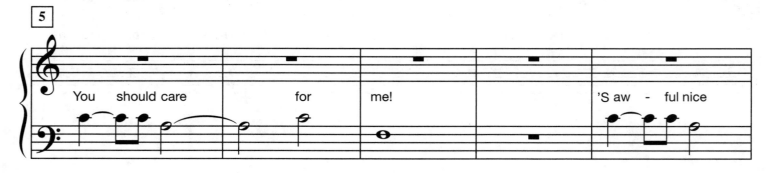

Optional Duet Accompaniment (Play solo part 1 octave higher than written.)

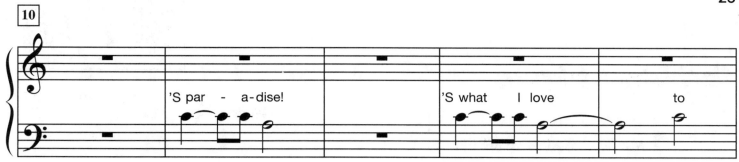

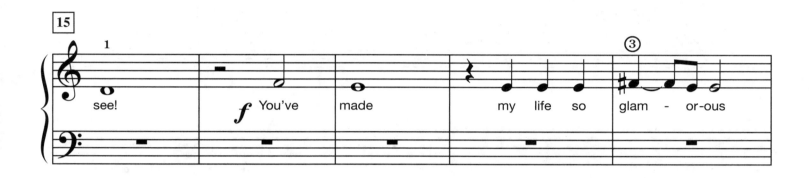

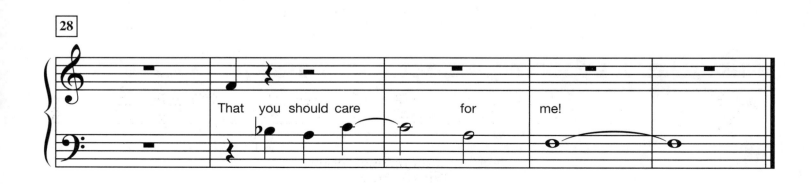

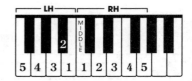

The Man I Love

Music and Lyrics by
GEORGE GERSHWIN and IRA GERSHWIN

Arr. by Tom Gerou

Some-day he'll come a-long, the man I love;

and he'll be big and strong, the man I love; and when he comes my way,

Optional Duet Accompaniment (Play solo part 1 octave higher than written.)

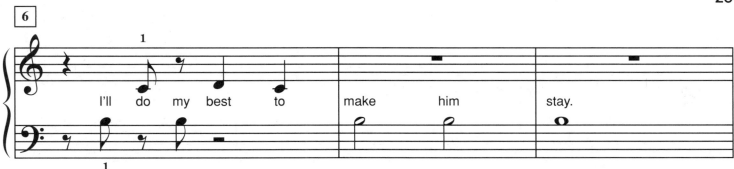

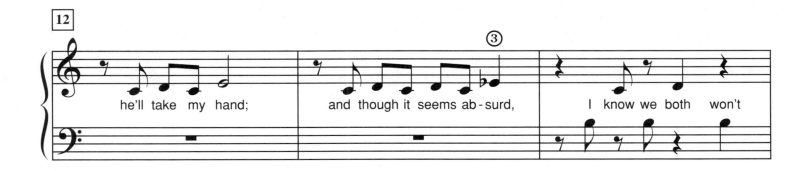

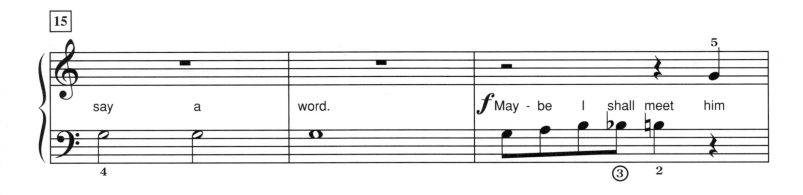

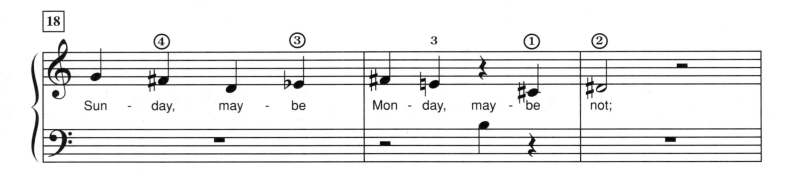

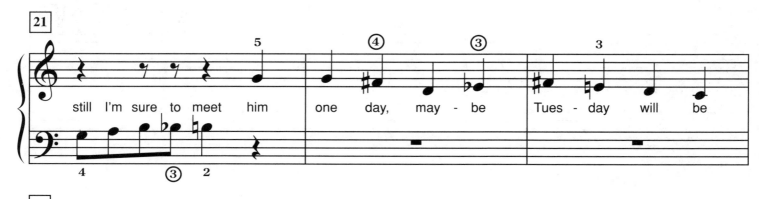

still I'm sure to meet him one day, may - be Tues - day will be

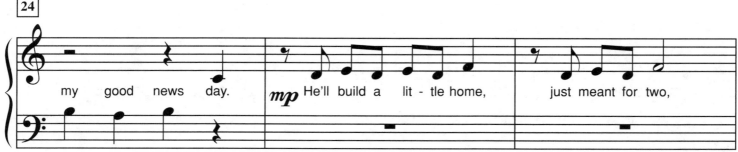

my good news day. *mp* He'll build a lit - tle home, just meant for two,

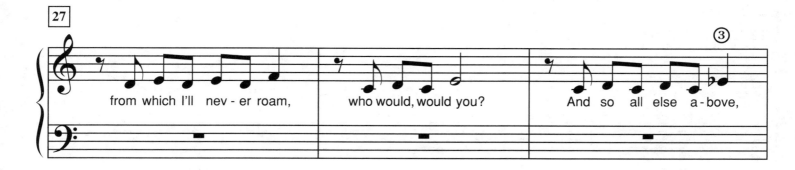

from which I'll nev - er roam, who would, would you? And so all else a - bove,

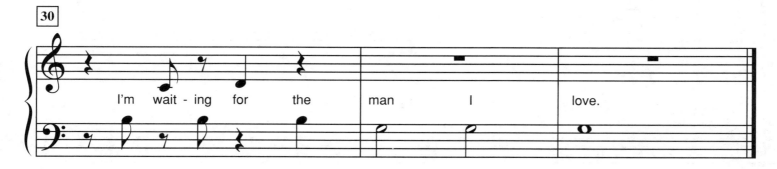

I'm wait - ing for the man I love.

(duet continued)

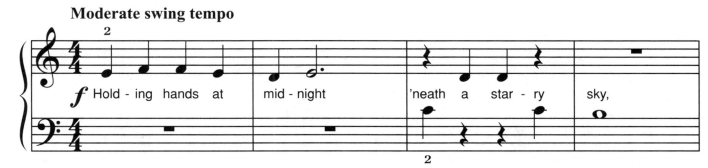

Nice Work If You Can Get It

Music and Lyrics by
GEORGE GERSHWIN and IRA GERSHWIN

Arr. by Tom Gerou

Moderate swing tempo

_f_ Hold - ing hands at mid - night 'neath a star - ry sky,

nice work if you can get it, and you can get it if you try.

Optional Duet Accompaniment (Play solo part 1 octave higher than written.)

Moderate swing tempo

_mf_ with pedal

9 Strol - ing with the one girl, sigh - ing sigh af - ter sigh,

13 nice work if you can get it, and you can get it if you try.

(duet continued)

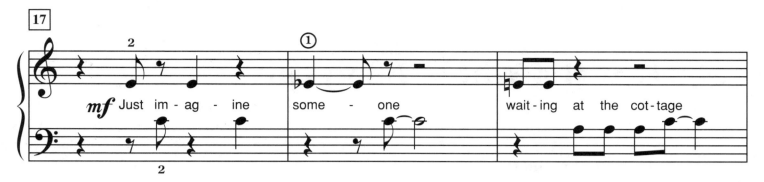

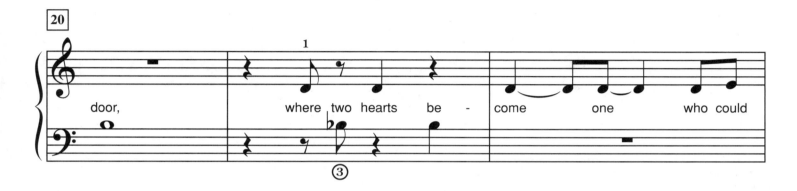

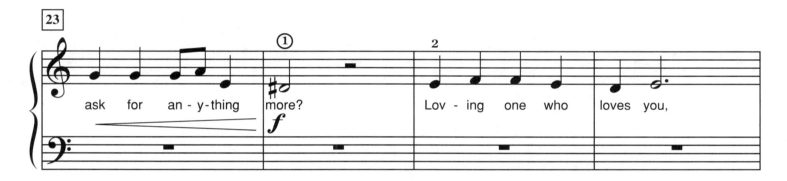

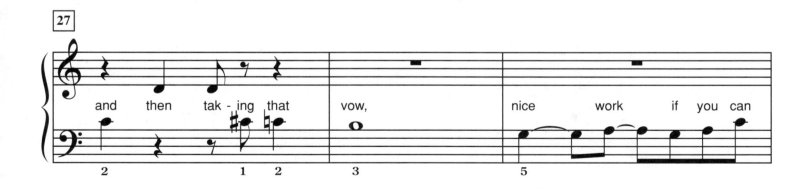

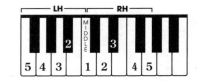

Let's Call the Whole Thing Off

Music and Lyrics by
GEORGE GERSHWIN and IRA GERSHWIN

Arr. by Tom Gerou

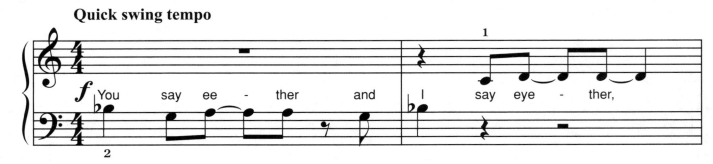

Optional Duet Accompaniment (Play solo part 1 octave higher than written.)

nee - ther, ny - ther, let's call the whole thing off!

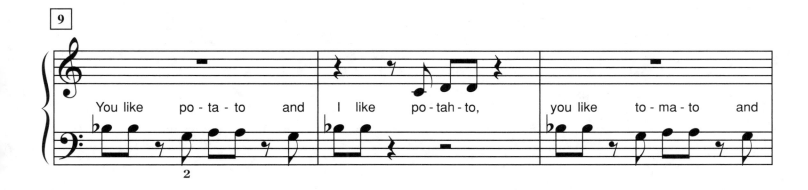

You like po - ta - to and I like po - tah - to, you like to - ma - to and

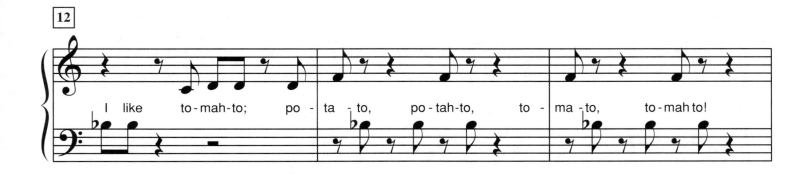

I like to - mah - to; po - ta - to, po - tah - to, to - ma - to, to - mah to!

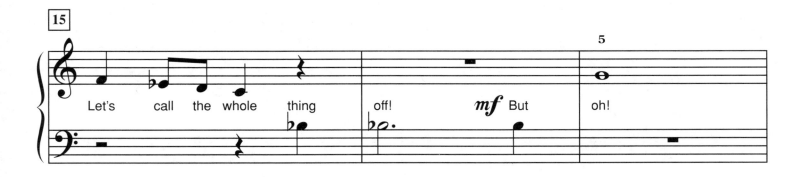

Let's call the whole thing off! **mf** But oh!

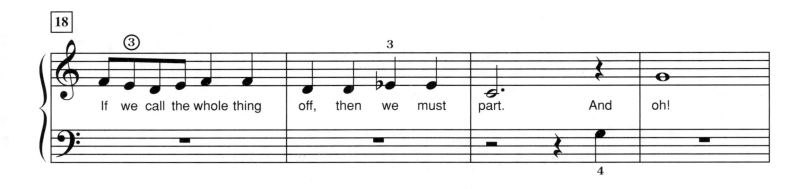

If we call the whole thing off, then we must part. And oh!

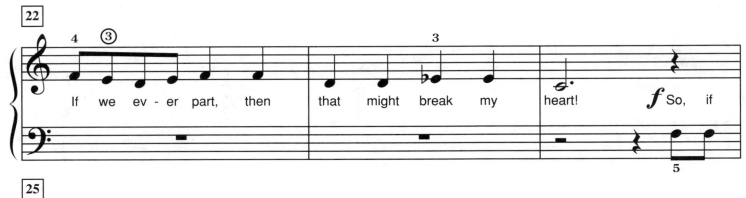

(duet continued)

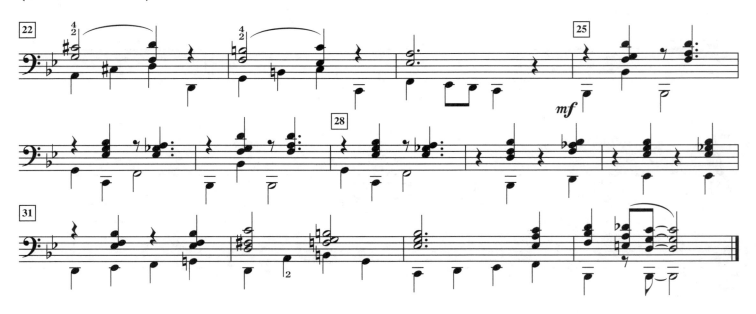